How to Become a Million-Dollar Producer

A Change in Your Paradigm

by

**Larry Klein
CPA/PFS, MBA, CSA**

© 2004 NF Communications, Inc. (800) 980-0192

All rights reserved. No portion of this book may be reproduced mechanically, electronically, or by any other means, including photocopying, without the express written permission of the publisher.

CONTENTS

Introduction 7

A Change in Your Paradigm 9

Change in Mindset 13

Million-Dollar Producers are Sales Professionals 14

The Fear 16

Hire a Service Assistant 17

Automate Your Marketing 18

Million-Dollar Producers Have Other People
    Bring Them Business 19

Hosts Who Can Bring You Business 22

Unlikely Hosts 23

Million-Dollar Producers Specialize 24

The Unique Selling Proposition and Target Market 24

Focus 26

The Unique Selling Proposition 28

Your Biography 29

Million-Dollar Producers Have a Programmed
   Revenue Stream 30

Big Producers Work On Their Business,
   Not In Their Business 32

Million-Dollar Producers Develop Their
   People (Sales) Skills 33

Make Your Initial Interview Different
   Than Anything They've Ever Seen 34

The Second Meeting 37

Ultimate Credibility 39

Action List 41

About Larry Klein 45

About NF Communications 47

Tools to Help You Become a Million Dollar Producer 49

INTRODUCTION

The financial advising business will get tougher. Why? Because your prospects are getting smarter. **Are you getting smarter, too?** Fifteen years ago, stockbrokers had an edge in that people had to call them for midday quotes. Financial professionals also had an edge, as they had product information and the prospect did not. That's all changed. If all you've got is product information, your days are numbered.

The broader your knowledge base, the more you stay one step ahead of your prospects. As they get smarter, so must you. If you stay wedded to selling only one product, don't be surprised if it gets harder to do business. People want advice. Not product advice, but rather, *financial advice.* Start giving it and start charging for it! (Addressed later.)

This is the millennium of self-learning. Those advisors who continually expand their knowledge base and apply what they've learned will win. Sadly, those who tread in one place will lose.

This book was written to help you establish and clarify your own unique approach, allowing you to distinguish yourself from every other advisor in town.

So let's get started.

How To Become A Million-Dollar Producer

A Change in Your Paradigm

To be a million-dollar-plus producer, you must think like an owner 100% of the time and not like an employee. Most advisors are caught somewhere in the middle. You realize you are in your own business, but you don't act like it. A business has structure, procedures, employees who do the work, and a way to consistently generate business. As the owner, your job is to design and manage this business, not to do the work.

But I know that if I were to come to your office on Monday, and you were the typical successful $300,000 to $500,000 producer, I would see little structure, a lack of written procedures, and a lack of adequate staffing. I would also witness you reacting to calls and to the market, and I'd see a lot of low-level activity on your part that does not produce revenue.

Most advisors are stuck at a low level of production because they do not understand that every business has "key success factors." When you focus on those factors, you make a ton of money. But most advisors use the wrong paradigm for their business, as they don't understand the key success factors of the financial advising industry.

To explain the key success factors of being a financial advisor, let's take a look at another industry.

In the automotive industry, for example, General Motors is the leader. It has 30% of the U.S. car market. What's the chance that they can increase that 30% to 60% next year? It's simply not possible. GM's growth is largely confined to the rate of growth in their industry. And since most people do not buy three or four cars, GM is pretty much constrained by growth that occurs within the driving-age population. At best, they are happy to grow their market share from 30% to 35% over the next decade by taking sales from their competitors.

In the short run, where should General Motors focus in order to maximize their profit? Since they can't impact revenue very much, they have far more influence over profits by managing their expenses. So in the auto manufacturing business, a key success to profitability is managing expenses.

he problem is, most financial advisors have the same focus. They too focus on managing expenses. However, managing expenses is NOT a key success factor of prospering in financial services. A key success factor is attracting more affluent clients, and attracting more affluent clients requires investing money.

If you are the most successful advisor in your town, you may have one-half of a percent of the market share of financial services there. Is it possible for you to double your share to one percent over the next year?

It's very possible for you to double your business, unlike what we saw with GM. Since the structure of your industry makes it easy to increase revenues (because your industry is highly fragmented), your focus should be on *revenue maximization, not cost minimization*. This means that you should seek to spend (invest) as much as possible in your business. You can take accounts away from the many other advisors in town. And since the financial services industry grows at double digits, there is a constant flow of business into the market.

The Right Business Model for Financial Advisors

	Few Sellers Concentrated	**Many Sellers Fragmented**
Slow Growth Market	Minimize Expenses	
High Growth Market		Maximize Revenue, High Investment

In my last year as a full-time financial advisor working for a large securities firm, I had employee business expenses of $70,000. The firm paid for my office, phone, business cards, and so on. My own expenses were for the marketing that I did and the assistant I paid that the firm did not reimburse. But you can tell me if it was worth it.

My gross commissions approximated one million dollars and I was the number-one producer in the office. The number-two producer had unreimbursed expenses of $30,000. The others had no unreimbursed expenses because they invested no money in their business. Seems to me that there is a correlation here between the amount of investment and the revenues generated.

Most advisors act like employees, not business owners, and they manage expenses and not revenues. They seek to spend as little as possible. Million-dollar producers manage revenues, not expenses.

So the first thing you need to do is change your paradigm. Seek to invest money, not save it.

The reasons you normally seek to save money are because you believe it is scarce. You have been trapped within this FALSE paradigm.

Here's the beauty of being alive in the 21st century; someone already knows whatever you want to know, and it's easy to find him or her on the Internet. If you have been lazy in seeking out experts, then I guess you have some work to do.

This is a century of self-learning. No one will call you up to give you the answers. The answers are there, however, for the taking. Million-dollar producers are self-learners. If a big producer wants to be an expert in direct mail, he reads books on direct mail and consults with an expert. In a short time, he too is an expert. And he makes profit with direct mail. Applied knowledge = money.

In my case, I wanted to become an expert speaker. I called the National Speakers Association and asked them to recommend their best coach. I called the coach and was told she charged $7,500 for two-and-a-half days of coaching. Most advisors would have been intimidated by the cost. But here's how big producers think: "I invest $7,500. I can earn an extra $10,000 per seminar. This is a great investment. Let's proceed."

Change in Mindset

When I was young, my mother told me to finish everything on my plate because people were starving somewhere (I can't remember if she told me Europe or China, but I doubt her assertion had any factual basis). She believed food was scarce, having lived through the Depression and seeing others go without.

You believe that money is scarce, time is scarce, and good clients are scarce. This is all a fallacy, and you bought into the same reasons unsuccessful people fabricate for being unsuccessful! How can money be scarce when there's a bank on every corner with a sign reading, "Borrow money here at super-low rates?" They even send you credit cards in the mail begging you to take their money. Money is not scarce! The only thing that could be scarce is *your ability* to attract money to you.

Unsuccessful people always think that the thing they want and don't have is "scarce." They go around saying things like, "Money doesn't grow on trees," "A penny saved is a penny earned," and "If I had a nickel for every time …."

There is plenty of money for you to attract, and investing in your business – and yourself – is one way to attract it.

And so it is with prospects and clients. There are plenty of prospects at this very minute with lots of money who are interested in good investments. As you've been reading this, thousands of people have made investments, and those people could become your clients. The only scarcity is your knowledge of how to attract them. So let's look at the formula for million-dollar production.

The formula consists of six basic elements that you are now ready to uncover.

Million-Dollar Producers are Sales Professionals

Most advisors are sales laborers. Here's the difference.

A **sales laborer** engages in activities such as:

- cold-calling
- setting up seminars
- servicing client problems
- writing a newsletter
- answering the phone
- sending literature
- doing research on the Internet
- opening mail
- scheduling appointments
- calling prospects

In contrast, a **sales professional** does the following:

- speaks at seminars
- has conversations with clients and prospects that result in revenue
- subcontracts the writing of a newsletter
- meets with organizations and people who can bring them new clients
- designs and documents procedures for assistants to implement

The activities you currently perform are the necessary activities to attain production at your current level. To get to the million-dollar level, you need to do *different* activities, not more of the same.

Sales professionals perform only professional activities and no clerical or administrative activities. In the financial advising business, there are three professional activities:

   a) Communicate with prospects about having them become clients
      i) You should not be doing the work of prospecting You are to get involved in prospecting only when a prospect has indicated interest

   b) Communicate with clients to retain them, or about doing additional business

   c) Design procedures for others to follow. You're the business owner, so it will always be your job to tell others what to do and lay out their work for them

Before we proceed, let's take a look at your local doctor's office so you can see these three activities in action.

When you call your doctor's office, does the doctor answer the phone? No, he has a receptionist (in the financial services business, we call this person a service assistant).

When you arrive for the appointment, does your doctor take your temperature and blood pressure? No, he has a nurse do that (in financial services, we call this person a sales assistant).

The doctor sees you ONLY when it's time to generate revenue. He gets involved in none of the non-revenue-generating activities of his practice (as you do in yours). As a result, he earns a lot more than you do. He is a professional, because he pays someone else to do the nonprofessional activities.

Why would any rational person (you?) not hire someone for $20 per hour when your time is worth $200 an hour? The next time you are about to make some crack about the financial knowledge of physicians, think twice, since it seems they know a lot more than you do about making money.

The Fear

At this point, some fear-based thought has entered your head, like: "I don't earn enough to get an assistant, but I know I could make more if I had one." You could spend your lifetime in that vicious circle. Here's the way out: Hire an assistant.

Borrow the money on your credit card, from your mother, or from your dog. Do whatever you need to do in order to get help, and stop doing clerical activity. By now you are thinking: "But how can I be sure that I can use the new spare time to generate enough new revenue to pay for the assistant?"

You can't be sure, but it's amazing how creative you get when you owe money. If you want to grow in your business, you'd better experience discomfort. As an American, the carrot does not motivate you; the stick motivates you.

So you will need to wield your own stick.

This is one of those universal laws. If you want to grow muscles and you go to the gym, you must experience discomfort. "No pain, no gain." In fact, your muscles grow when you injure them and they hurt! If you cut the tail off of a lizard, the lizard grows a new one. Why? Because pain=gain. Your business is no different! So if you want to be a million-dollar producer and get there comfortably, stop reading now and consider a government job.

Flip back to the list of activities that sales laborers do. Over the next 12 months, you will hire assistants or junior financial advisors to do these activities. You will spend your time only in the three activities that generate revenue, detailed on page 12.

Step #1: Hire a Service Assistant

These people perform the following activities:

- Answer the phone and handle 90% of the calls
- Send literature
- Do most client retention activities—birthday cards, holiday gifts, etc.
- Open mail
- Schedule appointments
- Handle client service issues and "follow-up"
- Handle the flow of paper

You find this person by placing an ad in the newspaper: "... administrative assistant—must be organized, meticulous and keep a clean desk."

This verbiage will screen out people who want excitement in their jobs. You can further screen any candidates by having them take a quick personality profile, excerpted from a book called "Please Understand Me." I have found these to be highly accurate.

Now what do you do with your new found free time? You do the second thing that million-dollar producers do....

Step #2: Automate Your Marketing

If you start each month wondering where your business will come from, there's good news: successful advisors don't do this. They have automated marketing that brings new clients every month.

In my case, I did one seminar a month. I invited 3,000 people, 50 to 60 people showed up, I had 20 appointments, and did business with 75% of these people. I was one of the top new account openers in my firm by spending 90 minutes a month giving a talk.

Note that I did not:

- stuff envelopes
- call people to invite them
- confirm their attendance

These are all laborer activities that I delegated to others. All I did was:

- give the talk
- meet with the prospects
- take their signed forms or checks

The next month, I simply repeated the same thing, over and over, all the way to the bank.

Million-dollar producers have such automated systems that bring new business without their worrying about it or spending their time maintaining the system. Seminars are only one way of doing this. There are many:

- Have someone make calls and set appointments for you
- Cultivate host-beneficiary relationships (more on this later)
- Advertise
- Run a direct-mail campaign

You may say, "I have run ads and used direct mail—they don't work." Is that why Proctor and Gamble keeps investing millions of dollars in direct mail and ads year after year? Your correct statement might be: "I don't yet know how to make direct mail work." So you hire an expert and find out.

Step #3: Million-Dollar Producers Have Other People Bring Them Business

In this section, I refer to other people who can bring you business as "hosts." You are the "beneficiary." Your goal is to set up many "host-beneficiary" relationships.

Your most important hosts are your clients. Million-dollar producers get more referrals from clients than smaller producers do. There are two items missing from your referral efforts. The first is you get an insufficient number of referrals.

The second is that you are merely getting names rather than introductions.

You were trained to ask for referrals in a variety of ways. Maybe to make your client feel guilty, or obligated, or with some approach like "I get paid in two ways: your commissions and your referrals." These are techniques from the 1950s.

Even when these techniques work, you get a name of someone that your client knows. The name is not worth much, because when you call them:

(a) they don't know who you are
(b) they don't know why you're calling
(c) they don't know why you were given their name

So instead of something of value, you are barely better off than if you had made a cold call. Let me suggest that you get an introduction rather than a referral. You can do this in a number of ways:

Have a birthday party or anniversary party for each of your 20 best clients. Tell them well in advance that you are throwing them a party at a restaurant. Have them invite four couples. For about $500 for the evening, you will be introduced to and get to know four couples who are like your best clients. If you did this all of next year for your 20 best clients, it would cost you $10,000. And you would meet 80 couples like your best clients, and you'd probably do a lot more than $10,000 in new business.

Another way is to have your clients send letters recommending you. I know a very smart planner who does this, but he does this as part of a whole system. Which leads to the second mistake made with most referral requests: you don't have a system.

Because you have no system, you ask your clients (when you remember to ask) or you end up asking too frequently or not enough. You do not set up a context for getting referrals.

One aspect of million-dollar producers is that they set up the context—the process—for accomplishing a goal. Most producers rush into the activity—the <u>content</u> without a <u>context</u>. The results they get are inconsistent and are usually not profitable. In a short time, they drop the activity and move on to pursue the next Holy Grail.

The million-dollar producer sets up a system. If he does not quickly get the results he wants, he tweaks the system. He tweaks it until he gets the desired result. He does not flit from tactic to tactic.

The smart planner I mentioned previously gets his clients to send an introduction letter for him. He has a detailed system.

When he starts a relationship with a new client, he asks, "What do I need to do so that in three months you will introduce me to your friends?" The client typically has reasonable requirements (keep in touch, don't lose me money, etc.). Three months later he calls them up and asks if he has fulfilled their desires. He then reminds them he'd like to be introduced to their friends as they promised. And he has a process where they willingly sign letters, some clients as many as 25, to their friends.

The letters are formatted so that they appear as personal communication from one friend to another, recommending their financial planner.

As a result, he converts 40% of those introductions to new clients. In fact, he is very selective now and only repeats this process with a few clients, as he only wants one new client a month that invests at least one million dollars with him.

(Visit http://www.nfcom.com/products/referral for more details on this system.)

Hosts Who Can Bring You Business

They approach CPAs with the basic pitch of "how about sending me some business." But nothing happens, because people, CPAs included, want you to answer only one question: "What's in it for me?"

So if you want referrals from CPAs, I suggest you do the following:

Each week, pick a CPA from the phone book. Call him and tell him you are a significant financial planner in town and that clients often ask you to recommend a CPA. Ask him if you can take him to lunch next week, to find out about his business and see if he would like some of these people as clients. Every CPA will agree to meet. Then spend most of lunch finding out about him and only the last few minutes talking about what you do.

Then the best way you will get referrals is to send the CPA some referrals first! You meet more people than he does, so every time someone asks about a CPA, don't just give out his name. Instead, call the CPA and ask him to get in touch with your prospect or client. Let him know you are working for him, and let him take control of the "sale" by calling the prospect himself.

I know one planner who cultivated relationships with just three CPAs. Combined, they send him one to two million dollars <u>a month</u> of new money to manage.

Unlikely Hosts

The hosts that can send you business are limited only by your imagination.

Larry Banks, a very smart insurance broker, wanted to sell long-term care insurance. It occurred to him that hospitals did a lot of marketing to seniors—free classes, blood pressure testing, community drives, etc. He called the hospital and asked if they would like to add a class on long-term care.

He now spends his time giving classes at hospitals, and has the hospital provide a meeting room where, for three days after the class, he meets with attendees and writes long-term care insurance. He is one of the largest LTC agents in the country!

So put on your creativity cap. Who already has clients just like those you want?

By working on your business and cultivating host-beneficiary relationships, you spend most of your day selling, not prospecting. That's why million-dollar producers can do more business in the same eight-hour day.

Step #4: Million-Dollar Producers Specialize

All advisors are saying the same things: "tax deferral is good," "save more for retirement," "buy and hold is the best strategy," "tax-free bonds are good for high-income investors," "this fund has a great track record," and so on. Is it any wonder that you do not appear special to prospects, that they have no compelling reason to do business with you?

This book is about learning how to look so distinctive from every other advisor in town, that your unique approach will be clear. Keep in mind that I am not recommending that you change anything about the substance of your business, but how you present it instead.

Think of it like this: isn't it true that one car advertisement can be so much better than the other? Yet both cars have a top speed of 100 miles per hour, the same gas mileage, and get you to your destination as well as the other car. But one car will outsell the other. Why? Because it is more successfully positioned in the mind of the buyer. That's what this book will do for you—put you in a superior position compared to other advisors.

The Unique Selling Proposition and Target Market

You need to summarize your business in one sentence—your unique selling proposition. That sentence must be like a laser that pinpoints your target prospect. That means you need to have a target prospect. So if your current prospect is "anyone with money," you're doomed. You can never grow a successful business without a target.

Your fear, of course, is that you will lose potential clients that are not in your target market. That's true. But you will gain five times as many of the prospects you seek. Let me share an example of this type of focus.

Early in my career, I had a position as a securities broker in a bank branch. I was assigned to nine branches. I would visit them all each week and the branch personnel would make appointments within the scheduled visit time. At some branches, there were more appointments than I had time available, and, at others, I would have idle time. Additionally, I wasted time driving between these branches.

So I told my manager that I did not want nine branches, I wanted only five. By reducing my travel time and focusing on these five more productive branches, my production doubled. After a few months, I told my manager I wanted only one branch, not five. I realized that by developing deeper relationships with the bank personnel at the biggest branch and by being there every day and being part of their team, I would get more referrals from them. I also realized that when the branch customers would see me every day, the familiarity and consistency would result in more business. My production doubled again by staying at one branch.

Note that my peers thought I was insane each time I requested fewer branches. They were all screaming for more branches (scarcity mentality). They of course thought that the more branches they had, the more prospects they would meet, the more potential they had and the more business they would do. While that thinking is logical, it's wrong; it ignores the benefits that come from focus and by targeting one's efforts.

By targeting my market and getting rid of lots of "potential," I was able to do a lot more business by converting a segment of the potential into more business. It's like getting married—you rule out lots of potential and focus your efforts. Most people find marriage a better choice than "having potential," as is evidenced by all of the people who get married each year and who want to get married.

Focus

When you get married, you get to know another person really well, and vice versa. That way, you always know what's pleasing to them. Do you remember when you were dating that one person who liked his/her ear licked and another person you dated who hated that? You probably were confused as to what your "prospects" wanted.

And that's the exact problem you will have if you do not focus on one target market. You will get confused, off-center, and you will not know the proper actions to take. If you talk to a baby-boomer in the morning, you will find he has a set of goals and concerns and needs to be approached in a very different way than you would approach his father as a prospect. In fact, the father and son will find different types of investments attractive (Junior is interested in an aggressive growth fund and Dad wants a fixed annuity).

By dealing with both groups, you will find that you have twice as many investments to track, you have trouble "getting into the heads" of both groups, and your sales closing ratio will be lower. You will spend more time at work juggling it all and you'll make less money. All because you are afraid that if you say no to all groups except your target market, you will lose potential clients.

In fact, you will gain clients, become more efficient, and you will know what your prospects think before they think it. You will deal with fewer investment products and services and will be able to document for your staff a set of repetitive processes and procedures that they can follow in your absence. Like when you leave the office at 3 p.m. every day to play nine holes!

Big producers work less than smaller producers. That does not mean you can leave your office now at 2 p.m. and suddenly make more money. Big producers are able to work less because their business is streamlined. Here's how they do it.

They have homogeneous clients. They don't meet with a 40-year-old who has stock options at 9 a.m. and then a wealthy retiree at 11 a.m. All of their clients are the same. They specialize by age, industry, occupation, or some other factor that makes each client similar to the other. As a result, they offer only a few products or services that fit the needs of all of their clients.

Every large producer has a target market or they are still working twelve-hour days and six days a week to keep up with their collage of different clients.

Smaller producers do business with everyone. So they try and keep track of 56 different mutual funds, 18 different annuities and 192 different stocks. That's inefficient and causes you to be in the office 12 hours a day. You have got to treat your business as an assembly line, not as a job shop.

Remember that we took a look at how your doctor runs his office? It's streamlined because he has the appropriate help, and if he is a specialist (like a cardiologist or oncologist), he sees the same problems again and again. And have you noticed that the medical specialists, just like the financial specialists, make the most money?

The Unique Selling Proposition

Only after you have limited your focus and decided on your target market can you define what you do for people. Currently, your unspoken selling proposition (shared by 90% of other financial service professionals) is "I help people invest money." Big deal. Who will that attract? It's not unique, and it's not a selling proposition (which must contain a benefit). Here's my Unique Selling Proposition (USP): "I manage investment portfolios for retirees so that they no longer need to worry about their money, have all the income they need, and pay less tax."

If a baby-boomer heard my USP he would have no interest in my services. And that's exactly the reaction I want. But if Mr. Smith, age 65 and recently retired, heard my USP, he'd want to know how I can help him. My USP attracts exactly the prospects I want. Notice that in constructing your USP, you really do not change the substance of what you do; you define your activities in a more focused way (which in turn, may lead you to offer particular products and services).

To summarize this section: If you want to differentiate yourself from every other advisor in town, have a UNIQUE selling proposition (one that sounds different from all the other advisors) and focus on one market. Clients want to deal with specialists, not generalists. Here's a graphic example:

A retired couple was on the same floor as my office to visit their CPA. They walked past my door, which says "Larry Klein, Certified Senior Advisor." They came into my office and asked my assistant exactly what I did, and they proceeded to make an appointment. My two meetings with them resulted in a $760,000 account. They told me, "We are so happy to have met you. We didn't want to deal with some young kid who wanted to gamble with our money. We wanted someone who knows about seniors, like us." To this day, they send me a holiday card each year, still gushing with their appreciation. That's the power of a USP.

Your Biography

You need to have a brochure or some printed piece that communicates how you are different and special. The main part of that piece is your biography. Biographies of most financial advisors sound alike. Here's how most advisors speak about themselves:

Bob Smith is a financial advisor at Jones and Peck. He helps people secure their futures with conservative investments and asset protection strategies. Constructing diversified portfolios of mutual funds, annuities and insurance, Bob helps his clients plan their financial future. He is a registered representative and holds an insurance license in Utah. He is a graduate of East Bum University with a degree in economics.

Now here's the biography of someone who focuses and commits to a specialized market:

Bob Jones is a well-known financial authority among affluent seniors. He has developed unique strategies to increase the income of people with $1 million-plus portfolios by more than 20% in a majority of cases. You may have seen his article in the Robb Report, "Even the Rich Like to Get Richer," or perhaps you've seen him as a guest on "Senior Money Matters" on KTDF-TV. Senior executives have used Bob's advice to cut their six-digit tax bills in half, pass on their estate completely tax-free and enjoy more spendable income. Bob is best known for his book, "Even the Affluent Deserve to Pay Less Tax."

When comparing these two biographies, you may think that Bob Jones sounds so much better because he knows more. However, he knows more about his target market because he focuses and does not get distracted. In fact, Bob Jones did not go to college as Bob Smith in the first biography did. But whom would you rather have as your financial advisor? (By the way, Bob Jones is not the great writer as his biography implies. He hired a financial writer to create the articles and book for him and he merely conveyed his ideas to the writer.)

Step #5: Million-Dollar Producers Have a Programmed Revenue Stream

I once read that IBM has 75% of their revenue programmed so that even if they don't make another sale this year, they still collect 75% of their revenues from ongoing activities like software licensing, maintenance contracts, upgrades and supplies.

Million-dollar producers also have their business programmed to generate revenue without constantly having to find new clients. This can be done in several ways:

The insurance sales professionals are getting continuous residuals (or should be). For example, on long-term care insurance, the typical residual is 10% annually. So when the client pays their $2,500 premium, the agent gets $250. If the agent sells 100 policies a year, by year 10 he has $250,000 coming in before he makes his first new sale that year.

The investment professional puts clients in "C" shares or places their portfolios under management. If he raises $10 million a year, after five years he collects $500,000 a year before bringing in a new client.

The smart annuity salesperson, although he gets paid up front, will not sell fifteen-year annuities. He will sell five-year annuities so that every year, he has annuities coming to term and a programmed revenue stream when they get exchanged or renewed.

Even a bond salesperson can generate such a stream. Some very successful producers do a lot of cold calling the first two to three years and develop a large list of affluent bond buyers (typically tax-free bonds). As a result, after this initial business establishment period, they are able to contact existing clients and move $500,000 of bonds a day (at a two percent commission). And bonds are always coming due and getting called. The nature of the client and nature of the investment creates a continuous revenue stream.

A substantial part of your business must be developing an ongoing revenue stream, unless you think you will be young forever and are willing to continuously work as hard as you do now.

Big Producers Work On Their Business, Not In Their Business

You will have occurrences in your business when you will think, "I know I can do it five times faster and better than my assistant." And rather than teach them, you will proceed to complete the task. And when the same thing occurs in three months, you'll end up doing it again. Remember that your time is worth 20 times more than the person you delegate to.

Therefore, you must always remember to work on your business, not in your business. Working on your business means:

- designing a new way of prospecting so that you get richer clients
- designing a new direct mail piece to increase the response rate by .5%
- finding a newsletter that will have a dozen people calling you each month

Let me tell you about Richard Heckmann, who worked on his business before he had any clients.

Dick had sold a business. He decided that being a stockbroker looked attractive. So he looked to see where all of the rich folks were, and saw that many retired to Palm Desert. (Dick also liked to golf, and the area has 100 golf courses.) So he moved to Palm Desert, bought a Maserati and joined the best country club.

The first friend he made was the head caddy. He always tipped him well and took him to dinner. Then he told him, "When I show up to play, put me in the foursome with the three richest guys at the club." So Dick shows up at 2 p.m. for golf and gets paired with three older gentlemen, two of whom are company chairmen, and the third, a retired and wealthy stockholder. After three holes, they can't stand it anymore and ask Dick how a 35-year-old guy can afford to be playing golf at 2 o'clock in the afternoon.

Dick says, "I'm a stockbroker and the market closes at 1 p.m."

"But don't you need this time to find new clients?" they ask.

"No, I get a lot of referrals."

"What exactly do you do?" they inquire.

"I write covered calls. Come by my office tomorrow morning at 10 a.m. and I'll show you."

Dick never had more than 62 clients, but he was the second largest producer at his firm. Every client was an exceedingly wealthy member of his country club or someone they referred. As you see, Dick mastered the art of working on his business, not in his business.

Step #6: Million-Dollar Producers Develop Their People (Sales) Skills

Sales skills are people skills. Yet it floors me that only 15% of the financial planners we have polled have had professional sales training. The other 85% are out there winging it. It makes no sense to have so much of your income depend upon sales conversations, yet you just hope for good luck every time you sit down with a prospect.

Selling is a SCIENCE, not an art. There is a structure to it that you can learn. And when you master it, you get rich. Salespeople (good salespeople) are the highest compensated people in the economy.

I am certain there are others, but Dale Carnegie and the Sandler Institute have sales classes across the United States. If you want to be a million-dollar producer, get trained in sales.

I was an accounting major and graduated to become a CPA. Another way to say this is I had no people skills. Although I wanted to be an actuary, my mother did not think I had the personality for it. I was the last person on earth who could excel as a salesperson. But I have, only because I—and you—can learn just about anything. I simply spent some time and money taking sales classes. So please, get trained.

Make Your Initial Interview Different Than Anything They've Ever Seen

Advisors constantly ask me if they can have a copy of my "fact finder" for the initial interview with a prospect. *Use a fact finder and you'll sound like every other advisor in town.*

To sound different than every other advisor, I recommend you follow the approach in Bill Bachrach's Values-Based Mastery kit or, in my firm's system, "How to Conduct a Prospect Interview and Close More Sales."

You have everyone bring a copy of their tax return and a copy of their investment statements to your initial interview. That way, there is no need to ask questions like, "How much income do you have?"; "From what sources do you receive it?"; "How is your money currently invested?" By having them bring the information, you can stop sounding like any other advisor they have consulted.

Your fact finding must be <u>emotional fact finding</u>. Questions such as:

- "How do you **feel** about that?"
- "Does that **worry** you?"
- "If we increased your income, how would you **enjoy** it?"
- "Tell me about your grandchildren." (Although there is no "emotion" word in this sentence, just watch their faces.)

You've probably heard many times that people buy emotionally and justify rationally. This means they make the purchase based on your tapping into their feelings. And when you ask appropriate questions about their feelings, a part of their brain will tell them, "This planner really understands me!" Your eventual recommendations will accommodate their feelings, rather than what you guess is important to them.

The first appointment must be focused on emotional fact finding. It's also what motivates them to meet with you again for your recommendations and to do business. At the end of the first appointment, you make a firm commitment for a second appointment and they will look forward to it! They will actually go home thinking, "This is great—I'm looking forward to his recommendations."

I recommend you charge a fee for preparing recommendations. To collect a fee you must be registered as an investment advisor with your State (a pretty simple process), or if your broker-dealer is a registered investment advisor, you simply sign on with them as a registered investment advis0r associate. Why is charging a fee important?

Because the prospect won't respect you if you don't. (Does their doctor or attorney do work for free?) And you must charge a fee to eliminate any tire-kickers before spending any time on analysis.

At the end of the first appointment, I say, "Mr. Smith, here's what I would like to do. I want to print out an independent report on each of your stocks and mutual funds so we can both see what's really going on. Then you'll know which to keep and which are doing you no good. Additionally, there are a couple ways to handle the estate tax issue, and I want to think about the pros and cons of each so that I can decide which is best for you. Last, I know we can increase your income by 20%, and I want to document for you a plan to do that. This will take five hours of my time, and my rate is $150 per hour. So if saving your kids $300,000 in estate taxes, increasing your income by $20,000 annually, and unloading investments that are hurting you is worth $750, then let's meet again next Wednesday."

If he says, "I'll think about it," either you have done a poor job of connecting in your emotional fact finding OR he is a tire-kicker. And you want to screen the tire-kickers out now. I promise you that if he has a hard time committing to your $750 fee, he certainly won't proceed when you deliver your recommendations to move his million-dollar account over to you.

The Second Meeting

At the second meeting, always "unsell" his current investments before you show your recommendations. Since most advisors just jump right into their program, you will show your superiority by showing that you have analyzed each of his current investments. Then recommend which should be held and which should be liquidated, and why.

Use independent services such as Morningstar, Value Line, and Vital Signs as evidence to show why you have reached these conclusions. Most advisors don't do this—they talk out of a posterior part of their anatomy instead. They spew their opinions that have no basis. You can be different.

Have you ever seen a legal opinion? The clients of attorneys pay large dollars for these opinions. The opinions fully document the research of the case law, the IRS code and court opinions. The legal opinions are based on evidence. Your recommendations must be the same in order to stand out.

If you think this sounds like a lot of work, it's not once you do it over and over. I rarely spend more than three to four hours in preparation for the second appointment, and, of course, I am collecting a fee for my time anyway, as will you.

Once you get agreement on your analysis of his current holdings, you proceed to your recommendations. But here's the key that separates you from every other advisor in town: You will state the pros and cons (positives and negatives) of every recommendation.

You need to make presentations as follows:

"So as you see, Mr. Smith, you really have a mishmash of funds here that overlap. You have focused too much on the same types of stocks and have been getting pretty lousy results. Do you agree? Let me make this recommendation. I have used, with great success, a diversification system using five mutual funds. These have been the benefits to my clients." (Enumerate the benefits.)

"Although the system has great benefits, you won't have any funds double in value in a year. So what happened to you three years ago with your biotech fund won't happen with one of these funds. They also will not fall 70% like your biotech fund, either."

"This is really the slow and steady route and not for investors who are seeking aggressive results because you won't get aggressive performance here. Is that okay with you?"

If you did your emotional fact finding correctly, you know that these "negatives" of your recommendations are music to his ears.

These "negatives" are actually benefits to him. But the important aspect is that no other advisor has ever given him the plusses and minuses.

Think about this. Have you ever been with a polished used-car salesman or a con artist? They tell you glowing things about their recommendation. Everything is not only positive, it's superlative. Financial advisors do the same thing and blow their credibility. Don't do that!

By explaining pros and cons, you are like the surgeon who explains the two different methods of correcting a problem to the patient and decides which one is best and asks for the patient's agreement.

You're a professional now, not a huckster!

By the way, it's not always the case that the "cons" are really "pros" to the prospect. But reveal all salient cons so that you can discuss them. That way, the client will not have surprises later and you won't hear "but you never told me that …." Even better, you won't get sued.

Ultimate Credibility

We live in a culture where writers are considered experts. Have you ever had a client bring an article from the newspaper and ask you to defend your investment recommendation when the article says the investment is not so good? Never mind that the person who wrote the article is a journalism major and never even took Finance 101. The journalist has far more credibility than you do because your clients believe that if it's in the newspaper, it must be true!

So here's how to get on this same prestigious footing. Be a writer. The good news is that you do not need to write anything. Our firm (as well as others) has written financial books, booklets and articles on which your picture, biography and contact information is printed.

Most people you provide the materials to will not even read it. They will see your picture and your biography on a book and will immediately reach the conclusion you must be an expert. Let me show you the power of this.

I have been working exclusively with senior clients during my career. I know all about how to do big production with seniors and help them with financial issues. But then I wrote a book called "Marketing Financial Services to Seniors." Just from some executives seeing this book, three huge insurance companies have called me to consult on their marketing efforts to seniors. I wasn't any smarter after I wrote the book, but I looked like an expert to the world. That's the power of your wisdom in print.

There is another angle I recommend for advisors: get interviewed in the newspaper. Then, you use copies of the articles for your clients to distribute to their friends as well as for you to give at seminars and to prospects. But how do you get interviewed?

First, get the name of the business editors at all of the local newspapers, radio stations and television stations in your area.

At least four times a year, you send a press release about some issue on which you have a unique opinion, data or service. You can learn to write a press release from books in the library or on the Internet. After sending two or three press releases, they recognize that you must be an expert and your phone starts to ring. I have been interviewed over two-dozen times doing nothing more than this.

Being someone who gets quoted in the press and someone who has written a book is not some distant fantasy. You can accomplish both in just a few weeks by getting outside assistance. (See www.nfcom.com/pr.htm).

Let's recap what you've learned about becoming a million-dollar producer, and let's make your action list:

Action List

1. You will seek to invest as much as possible in yourself and your business. What don't you know, that if you did know, would make you a lot of money? Find someone who knows this and have him or her teach you or get books and teach yourself.

    Have you had professional sales training? If not, then immediately enroll in a multi-week sales training where you learn the science of a sales conversation. Stop losing prospects to poor sales skills.

    Do you have an assistant? Get one.

    Do you have any hardware or software you need to improve your efficiency? Get it.

    You can double your income in a year, but it will never happen if you keep saving a few dollars here and there, thinking that saving money is the key to success.

2. You automate your marketing. If you do seminars, you no longer do them "when you're ready." You do them every month or every week.

    If you grow your business by referrals, you will implement a system to accelerate this process (visit www.nfcom.com/slroodman.htm).

    If you use direct mail, you will find every worthwhile book on direct mail, and become a master. You will find out the best type of envelope, paper color and day to mail. Direct mail, like every aspect of being a million-dollar producer, is a science, not an art.

Someone has already learned what works best, now just find out.

3. Decide what "hosts" you will cultivate to bring you business, and make a plan to spend a set time every week developing your hosts.

4. Decide which market you will serve. Serve only that market and become a specialist. (Make sure your market has money.) Decline or refer away business that comes to you from outside your selected market. Hire a junior rep to handle the existing clients you have outside your selected market. From now on, you are one mean, lean, focused, laser-guided machine.

5. Write down the programming of your revenue stream. For example:

I will sell 10 long-term care policies per month at $2,500 annual premium. At the end of year one, the annual residual on these polices is $30,000. I will do this for 10 years and have an income of $300,000 annually in year 10 before I sell a policy.

6. Select a three-hour slot per week to be out of your regular workplace to work ON your business.

7. Structure, on paper, how you will pursue a prospect interview. Use one of the models mentioned in the book, or you may develop your own. Realize that meeting with a prospect is not "let's see what happens," but, rather, a predetermined process that maximizes your probability of getting a new client.

8. Get press. Get interviewed in the newspaper or have a book written. Nothing convinces people to do business with you like handing them your book.

If you need a little more inspiration, read "Marketing to the Affluent" by Tom Stanley. It's a collection of stories about extraordinary sales professionals.

Realize from this moment on that any inspiration or knowledge you need is on the Internet, in a book, or has otherwise already been discovered by someone else. Simply get that resource to go anywhere you want.

About Larry Klein, CPA/PFS, MBA, CSA

Larry Klein, President of **NF Communications**, has assisted over ten thousand financial professionals to increase their clients and income. His marketing programs, tested in his own practice, are offered to financial professionals throughout the United States (www.nfcom.com).

Mr. Klein started his career as a CPA with a Big Eight accounting firm and moved into advising retail clients as a Vice President of Investments at Great Western Financial Securities and then as a First Vice President and branch manager with Prudential Securities (where he was in the top 5% of producers). In 1987, Registered Representative Magazine, the leading trade journal for the stock brokerage industry, selected Larry as one of the **Ten Outstanding Investment Brokers in the United States**.

Mr. Klein is a CPA, a Certified Senior Advisor (one of 8,000 in the U.S.), a Registered Investment Advisor, and he holds an MBA from Harvard Business School. His latest book, Marketing Financial Services to Seniors, is available at www.nfcom.com.

Larry has lectured widely on financial topics at Boston University, the University of San Francisco and the University of California at Berkeley. He has written dozens of articles on financial topics spanning estate planning, retirement plans and Social Security.

He has been interviewed in industry publications, including On Wall Street, Registered Representative Magazine, The Agent's Sales Journal, Viewpoint—the Magazine for CNA Agents, and Financial Advisor Pro, and writes columns for Financial Services Journal Online (http://fsc.fsonline.com/fsj/) and Horsesmouth (www.horsesmouth.com).

In these industry publications, he counsels financial services professionals on how to use smart and efficient seminars, direct mail and direct response marketing to obtain substantial increases in their income.

He is author of <u>Retirement Investing</u>, <u>Asset Protection and Wealth Preservation</u>, <u>400 Greatest Financial Jokes</u>, <u>Marketing Financial Services to Seniors</u> and a number of booklets on financial topics for senior investors. He has spoken at many professional venues, including the Charles Schwab Advisor Conference, the 2001 NAIFA Financial Advisors Forum and the Million Dollar Round Table.

About NF Communications, Inc.

Do you have enough clients? Enough *wealthy* clients?

Acquiring clients can be difficult or easy. It's easy when you use the same process as top producers. NF Communications, Inc. packages the marketing systems of top producers and makes them available to all planners who want to quickly grow their business. These systems are designed and field-proven in actual practices of highly successful planners.

- Want to know how to fill the seminar room with qualified attendees without feeding people dinner?

- Want to close appointments right at the seminar?

- How about a newsletter that gets you twenty responses every month?

- Would you like to run an ad that has twenty to thirty people calling you?

- How would you like to be an author overnight?

- Want to know how to find and target existing annuity owners for exchanges and conversions to life policies?

- Find out how to attract qualified prospects for estate planning and actually have them take action.

- Learn how to attract 401(k) rollovers.

Each of these systems provides access to conference calls with the creator of the system so that you can implement it just as the top producer uses it. Never be in need of new clients again.

48

Tools to Help You Become a Million Dollar Producer

Raise $1 Million Per Month Seminar System

Build a $50 million book in under five years using cost-effective seminars. If you are tired of low attendance, lack of confidence in your speaking skills, or too few appointments, we'll show you how to fill up the room and close appointments right at the seminar! Most important, you will learn how to solve the biggest problem—you will learn how to fill up the seminar room every time and never have low attendance again. You will learn how to raise $1 million per seminar.

Included is a seventy-five-minute video of a recent seminar, and you'll see it all! Seminars are the fastest, easiest way to generate lots of new clients, and we'll show you how to open fifteen new accounts a month. This is designed for stockbrokers, fee-based advisors, and financial planners.

There are several seminar topics to choose from. Each presentation is a generic seminar designed for prospecting the senior market (age sixty-plus)—where all the money is. It shows your audience the financial mistakes they make and why they need to come see you. And you'll see how to close the appointments right at the seminar.

Seminar System with Personal Coaching
Call for current pricing
90-Day Guarantee* NASD Reviewed

*conditions apply, call for details. System components and specifications subject to change without notice.

Estate Planning Seminar System

Would you like to have a lot more affluent clients, and would you like to sell large insurance policies and gather significant portfolios for money management? That's what this seminar package will do for you.

We show you the method for attracting attendees who have estate-planning problems that you can solve. Most important, we give you a seminar presentation that will motivate the attendees to act. Many producers find that it's hard to get people to move forward on estate-planning issues. That's because these producers are focusing on how much the kids can save in estate taxes. In this program, you will show the parents—your clients—what's in it for them. You will show them how to eliminate capital gains tax, increase their cash flow, and reduce their income taxes, all as part of their estate planning.

You will not be talking technical mumbo jumbo as many attorneys do. You will be talking in plain English that motivates the attendees to make an appointment with you before they leave the seminar room.

Estate Planning Seminar System with Personal Coaching
Call for current pricing
90-Day Guarantee *

*conditions apply, call for details. System components and specifications subject to change without notice.

For more information or to order, call 1-800-980-0192, option 4
or visit **www.nfcom.com/million**

Sell Two to Four Additional Annuities Per Month

Sell two to four large annuities a month using small, inexpensive ads. The ads bring you people who already own annuities. You are able to do lots of 1035 exchanges and convert some of these to life policies (to avoid the tax time bomb), making you a very handsome commission. While most advertising systems generate high volumes of low-quality leads, this system generates a low volume of high-quality leads so you don't waste your time. We show you where to get a list of existing annuity owners and direct mail to them and where to run inexpensive ads to attract affluent seniors.

If you want to sell more annuities, you have got to see the details of this simple system that works.

Annuity System with Personal Coaching
Call for current pricing
90-Day Guarantee* NASD Reviewed

*conditions apply, call for details. System components and specifications subject to change without notice.

For more information or to order, call 1-800-980-0192, option 4
or visit **www.nfcom.com/million**

Have Your Own Financial Book

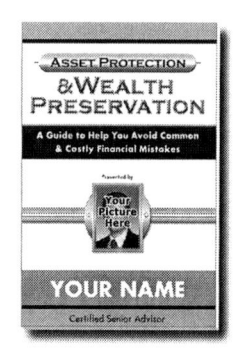

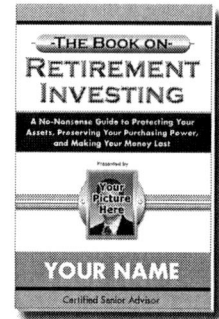

How would you like to have the credibility of an author? You can! We will write your book for you. Our professional writers turn your ideas into your own unique, published masterpiece. Or here are three easy-to-read, generic books on financial topics of interest to seniors. We can print the books with your name, picture, and biography. How do you think the prospects will react when you hand them a copy of your book? We show you ten ways to use your book to quickly gain more clients.

This is the easiest way to build your credibility and differentiate yourself from every other broker, planner, and advisor in town.

Call 1-800-980-0192, option 4 for pricing, information on protected territories or to receive a free sample of a book.
NASD Reviewed

For more information or to order, call 1-800-980-0192, option 4 or visit **www.nfcom.com/million**

Direct-Response Newsletter

Each month, send a newsletter to clients and prospects, and each month get ten to twenty replies asking for more information. That's right—ten to twenty people ask you for more information or appointments about investment opportunities. You may use some lame newsletter merely as a public relations tool. How would you like to see it pay for itself with measurable results? Take a look at using a newsletter that helps you make more sales and directly generates profits.

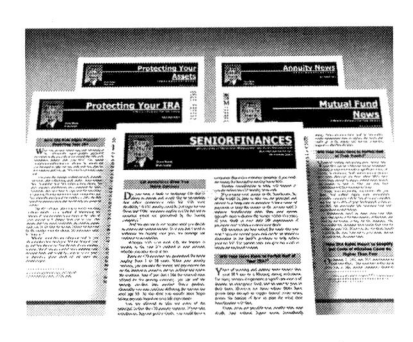

Most importantly, this newsletter helps you convert those prospects who come to your seminars or meet you, but never take action. When they keep getting your newsletter, they never forget you. When they're ready, you're the one they call because you're the one who's been there. It's the best return you'll ever have for such a low cost per prospect.

Each month you get the newsletter contents via email – just drop in your picture and print as many as you want for a single low monthly fee.

Call 1-800-980-0192 option 4 for current pricing
Each Article NASD Reviewed

System components and specifications subject to change without notice.

For more information or to order, call 1-800-980-0192, option 4
or visit **www.nfcom.com/million**

Mechanical Money-Management Strategy

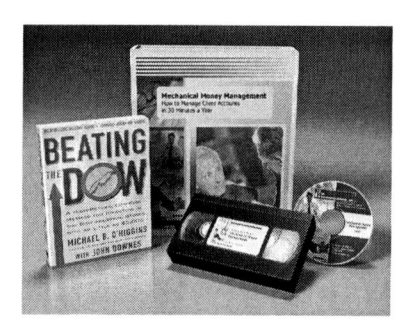

Would you like to raise a lot more money for money management? It's easy when you show prospects how they mess up their own portfolios. They have no system and are constantly shooting from the hip after watching CNBC or reading Money magazine. Worse, even their brokers have no strategies for them to follow.

Americans invest based on whim and fleeting opinion. When you show prospects how you use a mechanical system to invest, they will see that you have a discipline and you are the professional they should trust. And you'll have a lot more time when you have all of your client portfolios on a mechanical system that needs to be rebalanced only once annually. You will learn how to present these systems at a seminar and one-on-one and have prospects opening new accounts with you.

We show you how to present the Dow Dividend Strategy and the Value Line Strategy, as well as how to use these systems to turn your practice into a well-oiled machine.

If you like the idea of commissions (or fees) every year, retaining clients, and doing little work, then this system is for you. It's the fastest, easiest way to manage clients' money and deliver great performance without watching the stock market. This is also a great way for those who have little stock market experience (life agents or series 6 licensees) to start managing clients' money with great results.

Mechanical Money-Management System with Seminar Video Presentation - Call for current pricing.

System components and specifications subject to change without notice.

Advanced IRA Distribution Strategies Seminar System

You will learn to identify and attract those investors with $250,000 or more in their retirement plan or IRA. In 90 minutes you will introduce three strategies, two of which other planners and CPAs don't even know about.

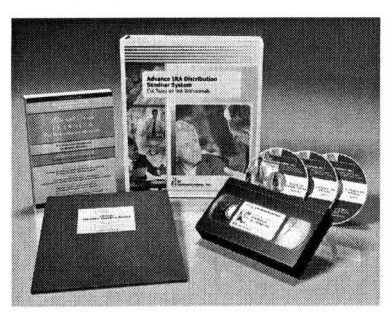

While other planners waste time discussing the new minimum distributions rules vs. the old (which the clients' custodian takes care of anyway), you'll be adding value by showing attendees why you're head and shoulders above their current advisor.

**Advanced IRA Distribution Strategies
Seminar System with Personal Coaching**
Call for current pricing.

System components and specifications subject to change without notice.

For more information or to order, call 1-800-980-0192, option 4
or visit **www.nfcom.com/million**

LTC/Medicaid Seminar System

Sales of long-term care insurance are soaring! If you're not tapping this market, you are missing one of the greatest insurance growth markets of the decade. Use this program to attract seniors to appointments. But the seniors are tired of the sales pitch and have heard it too many times. How can you reach them and get them to listen?

This seminar package will show you how. You'll not only make long-term care sales (commissions to 75 percent and great residuals), you will also see how to sell annuities for Medicaid qualification as well as capture investment business.

Long-term care is the hottest topic for insurance agents to open the door to lucrative senior appointments.

Long-Term Care Seminar System with Personal Coaching
Call for current pricing.
90-Day Guarantee* NASD Reviewed

*conditions apply, call for details. System components and specifications subject to change without notice.

For more information or to order, call 1-800-980-0192, option 4 or visit **www.nfcom.com/million**

An Annuity Seminar System That Works!

It took three years of development, but we finally have an annuity seminar that is compelling enough to fill the room. The seminar is presented as Nine Ways to Cut Your Taxes. It shows attendees nine techniques to reduce their taxes – seven of the methods are with annuities, the other two are with life insurance. That's a win-win situation for both you and the client!

The system includes video and audio of an actual seminar so you can see how it's done. We'll teach you how to host the seminar at the lowest cost, fill up the room with affluent attendees and close appointments right at the seminar.

If you've been searching for an annuity seminar that generates immediate sales, then this is the one for you!

Annuity Seminar System with Personal Coaching
Call for current pricing.
90 Day Guarantee* NASD Reviewed

*conditions apply, call for details. System components and specifications subject to change without notice.

For more information or to order, call 1-800-980-0192, option 4
or visit **www.nfcom.com/million**

Personalized Booklets for Instant Credibility

The quickest way to indicate your expertise is with your wisdom in writing. But writing can be very time consuming. So NF Communications offers booklets that you can send to prospects and clients, booklets that are personalized with your name, picture, biography, and contact information on the cover!

Annuity Owner Opportunities (17 pages)—a motivating booklet that shows existing annuity owners the mistakes they make and the knowledge they lack. **Articles include**: 
- Are You Stuck in a Low-Rate Fixed Annuity?
- Will You Lose 50% of Your Annuity Value to Estate and Income Taxes?
- An Annuity That Rises with Stocks
- Annuities Can Help Reduce or Eliminate the Tax on Your Social Security Benefits
- Income for Life

Seven Ways Retirees Can Cut Taxes (18 pages)—this booklet highlights the virtues of annuities and VUL with these articles: 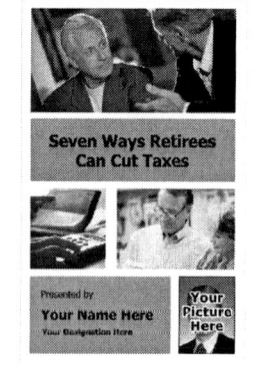
- Fixed Immediate Annuities - A Little Understood Tax Saver and Income Booster
- A Better Alternative To Tax-Free Bonds?
- Do You Pay Tax on Social Security Income?
- Why Defer Tax if you Have to Pay it Anyway?
- Potential Tax Relief For Mutual Fund Investors

Personalized Booklets for Instant Credibility

Mistakes in Selecting Mutual Funds (18 pages)—mutual fund owners think they know what they're doing. But once they read this, they will understand why they need to meet with you. Topics covered:

- Beware of Last Year's Best Funds
- Mutual Fund Fees
- Taxes
- Turnover
- Derivatives and Style Drift
- Putting Together a Mutual Fund Portfolio

Avoid Mistakes Buying Long-Term Care Insurance (17 pages)—show your prospects that you're not just another long-term care salesperson—you'll actually show them how to avoid mistakes in making this important purchase. Articles include:

- Do You Need Long-Term Care Insurance?
- When Should You Get Insurance?
- Two Important Reasons to Get Long-Term Care Insurance
- Five Ways to Reduce the Cost of Long-Term Care Insurance
- Which Insurance Company is Best?

For more information or to order, call 1-800-980-0192, option 4 or visit **www.nfcom.com/million**

Personalized Booklets for Instant Credibility

IRA Distribution Mistakes and How to Avoid Them (19 pages)—this booklet is designed to accompany our Advanced IRA Distribution Seminar System and can be used by any planner interested in this area. The articles include:

- Never Take More Than Your RMD
- Why the Stretch IRA May Be Doomed to Fail
- How Your IRA Custodian May Cause Problems
- Mistakes in Selecting Beneficiaries
- Sheltering Your Retirement Money from Estate Tax
- Use Life Insurance As A Transfer Vehicle (In a Qualified Plan)

CD Shoppers' Guide (13 pages)—this booklet covers these topics:

- Where to Obtain Paying CDs
- Callable CDs
- Index-Linked CDs
- FDIC Insurance—Do You Really Understand It?
- Are Fixed Annuities a Good Alternative to CDs?
- Are Your CDs Titled Correctly?

For more information or to order, call 1-800-980-0192, option 4 or visit **www.nfcom.com/million**

Increase Your Closing 20 Percent Sales Presentation System

Often, when the prospect doesn't buy, isn't it a close call? Wouldn't just a little more of "something-that-you-can't-figure-out" have converted that prospect into a client? If you think about it, the fastest way to increase your income is to close those sales that get away. It takes no more of your time and you don't need to see more prospects. Just a different approach in the sales process can substantially increase your results. Such an approach is available to increase your closing ratio.

This system ensures you spend your time with people who move forward and become clients. This system harvests those prospects who are "close calls" and turns them into clients.

You get videos of sales situations so you can see and hear just what to do. Plus you'll learn how to read a tax return to uncover more business opportunities with the prospect.

Video Sales Presentation System
Call for current pricing.

System components and specifications subject to change without notice.

For more information or to order, call 1-800-980-0192, option 4
or visit **www.nfcom.com/million**

How to Double Your Income As a Fee-Based Money Manager

Want to capture the trend of fee-based management? Not sure how to transition your clients? Not sure how to work with new prospects on a fee basis? We'll teach you everything you need to know to create a mountain of residual fee income. No more starting from zero on January 1st. Wealthy clients want fee-based relationships and they are concerned about potential conflict of interests in commission relationships. We also teach you how to cultivate these affluent relationships and manage investment portfolios better than 89% of the portfolio managers (and we've got the data to prove it).

Go with the market trend to fee-based management before your commission business disappears.

This deluxe package includes 1) your choice of any one of our seminar systems, 2) Money Management System, 3) six months of the Direct Response Newsletter and 4) Personal Coaching.

Deluxe Program
Call for current pricing.
90-Day Guarantee*

*conditions apply, call for details. System components and specifications subject to change without notice.

For more information or to order, call 1-800-980-0192, option 4 or visit **www.nfcom.com/million**

Never Prospect Strangers Again!
Client Introduction System

We've tossed out all the wrong things you've been taught about referrals and show you the three elements of getting referrals to end all other prospecting.

We have a proven system that really works and has been tested and tested. You can easily turn 100 clients into 400 clients or more in two years. A lot of referral systems are based on the personality of the person that came up with it, and it doesn't work for many other people. But this system works for anybody.

You learn:

- How to get an introduction to each referral
- How to warm up the referral before you contact them
- How to build on each referral for additional introductions

Here's what one recent system owner said: *"Just thought I'd let you know, I recently ordered your Client Introduction System. I followed your instructions to the letter, watched the video and called two clients to test the process out. I am happy to say the system worked like a charm. In a low-key, easy fashion I now have 50 introductions. I guess I will be very busy in December! This system is unbelievable - simple and effective."* Jack K., Anaheim, CA

You get the complete workbook plus a video showing you exactly what to do and say each step of the way. Just follow the simple, non-threatening, non-embarrassing steps and you'll never have to prospect strangers again.

For more information or to order, call 1-800-980-0192, option 4
or visit www.nfcom.com/million

Just One Idea from These Big Producers and Financial Marketing Experts Can Explode Your Production

Watch these videos and you'll learn how to become a top financial producer. Just one idea from them can easily put $50,000 in your pocket, if not double your income.

We know that not every idea you hear will fit your personality or your business. So we've lined up fifteen great presenters, each with a dozen ideas that can make the difference in your business, get you off that production plateau, and have your colleagues wondering how you made such a big jump in income so fast.

Smart producers don't reinvent the wheel—they copy it. If you're a financial planner, stockbroker, life agent, or investment advisor wanting to blow the doors off your production, you have got to listen to these experts!

You can choose from a variety of topics and speakers to suit your interest. Each comes with video, audio and speaker notes.

For details and to order, visit
www.4-financial-advisors.net

For more information or to order, call 1-800-980-0192, option 4 or visit **www.nfcom.com/million**

Financial Jokes

Get your point across better with humor. Here's the book for you: 400 Greatest Jokes for Financial Professionals. When you add humor, you will close more appointments from seminars and more sales from presentations.

This book has jokes and stories about the stock market, investing, health care, CPAs, attorneys, bankers, stockbrokers, technology, money, marriage, estate planning, insurance, and patience. Afraid that you can't deliver a joke well? Don't worry, an audio CD is included that teaches you how to employ the four most important aspects for telling great jokes.

Lighten up your presentations with a little humor and watch your sales take off!

**Joke Book plus Audio CD
on How to Deliver a Great Joke**
Call for current pricing.

For more information or to order, call 1-800-980-0192, option 4
or visit **www.nfcom.com/million**